Fashion DRAWING STUDIO

A guide to sketching stylish fashions

D0301046

3114150

TABLE OF CONTENTS

Harajuku

Hollywood

ROCK STAR

SKATER CHIC

Drawing to design

STEP 1: Start with a simple line drawing. Pick your favourite pose, and use light guidelines to build your model.

STEP 2: Darken the outlines, and start adding in details like hemlines and hand placements.

STEP 3: Erase guidelines, and draw in things such as fabric prints, hair, facial features, and accessories.

STEP 4: Finish any final details and then add in colour, textures, and shading to bring your model to life.

Clothes are more than pieces of fabric used for warmth. Societies around the world and throughout history have used clothing as a statement. Clothing can be used in many ways and for many purposes – as a political statement, for example. Clothing is also used to express the customs and culture of local people. It represents changing times or events from the past. And it can be beautiful.

Fashion can be as simple as a popular look, like "girly girl". It can represent the style of a country or region, like "all-American girl" or "Harajuku". It can show off a person's interests, like "skater chic". It can give us a glimpse into the lives of the rich and famous, like "rock star" and "Hollywood".

Fashion illustrators use their talents to show off the latest clothing styles and designs. But fashion illustration is also a form of artistic expression. The colours, lines, shapes, and techniques used are unique to each illustrator. Whether it's a quick runway sketch or a full-colour drawing used for an advertisement, a talented illustrator can bring a model to life.

As you flip through the pages of this book, think about how you can add your own personal style. Draw the models your way. Use what art style works best for you. Invent your own fabrics, textures, and prints. Don't forget – these are fun fashions YOU can sketch!

Follow these tips for a fun fashion experience:

- Sketching allows you to make any major changes before adding colour or details. Ink pens will give your sketches a more finished look.
- Experiment with different art mediums. Markers and coloured pencils are fun, but don't forget about watercolour paints and pencils, pastels, permanent markers, and charcoals.
- Give digital art a try. There are many free or inexpensive apps for smartphones or tablets.
- Adding 3-D effects, such as glue, glitter, diamanté, and collage, will help your art pop.
- Use what you draw! Hold an art show to show off your pieces. Or, better yet, bring your outfits to life and have a fashion show with your friends.

Sweet simplicity

A sweet cardigan and cute capris are a great look for an all-American girl. The trick is turning an everyday outfit into something flirty and feminine.

TIP: Don't go overboard with this one. Pair your favourite girly print with simple, solid colours.

Coordinated
couture

Suit up for style with an all-American girl twist. Pencil skirts are timeless – make yours modern with bright colours and patterns. A jacket with a wide collar draws the eye to a confident girl who's going places.

TIP: While matching is great, you don't want to overdo it. Pair a coordinated outfit with a flashy bag that complements your chosen colours.

Dip-dyed diva

Can't make it to the tropics? Bring the summer sun to you! Warm tones give a tiered dress an exotic look and a bright splash of colour. Cool things off with a crocheted jacket and some sharp boots.

TIP: Try using a single colour to create different layers and shades to the dress.

The great outdoors

Explore the great outdoors and look good doing it! Choose soft checks and familiar shorts for comfort and style. Stash accessories in a stylish yet rugged rucksack.

TIP: Checks come in many colours and styles. Experiment with a wide variety of prints to find your favourite.

NEW WEST

Turn the Old West into something new. A trendy vest cinched with a glittering diamanté belt is a start. But adding a cowboy hat, a hot handbag, and some blingy pendants will show how the West was won.

TIP: Don't be afraid of the Wild West. Fringe, ruffles, distressed denim, leather, vests, and boots are just a few style additions to bring to this outfit.

Natural earth tones

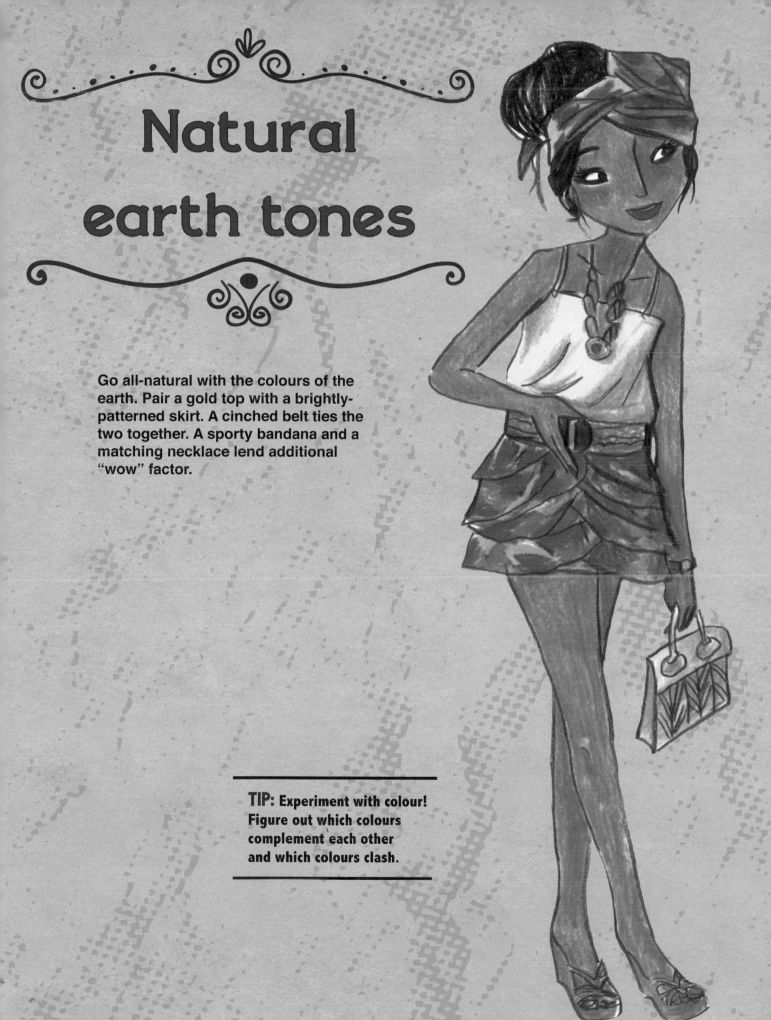

Go all-natural with the colours of the earth. Pair a gold top with a brightly-patterned skirt. A cinched belt ties the two together. A sporty bandana and a matching necklace lend additional "wow" factor.

TIP: Experiment with colour! Figure out which colours complement each other and which colours clash.

HOME TEAM

Do you run the bases or watch from the sidelines? Use this American pastime as fashion inspiration and you're always a winner. The crowd will be rooting for the home team!

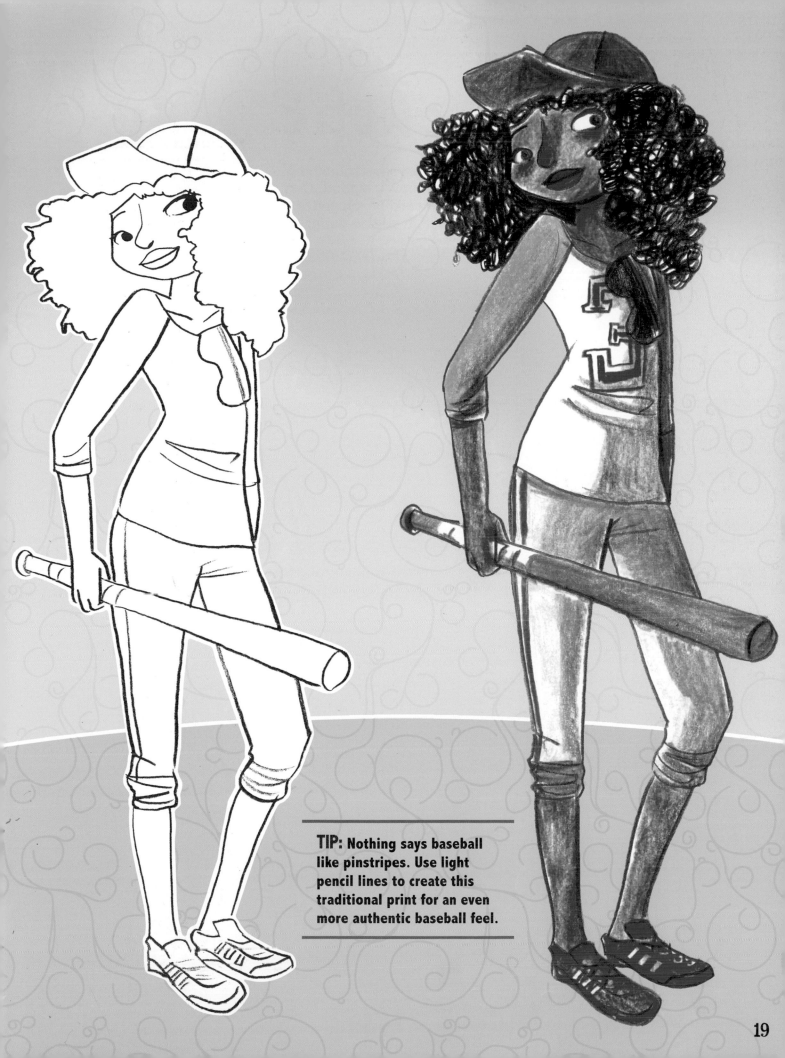

TIP: Nothing says baseball
like pinstripes. Use light
pencil lines to create this
traditional print for an even
more authentic baseball feel.

An ono outfit

When a Hawaiian says something is "ono", you know it's good! Get inspired by Waikiki beach and dress yourself in an ono outfit.

TIP: Hawaiian style is more than leis, coconuts, and hula skirts. Bright colours, loud prints, and natural fibres are more in touch with island fashion.

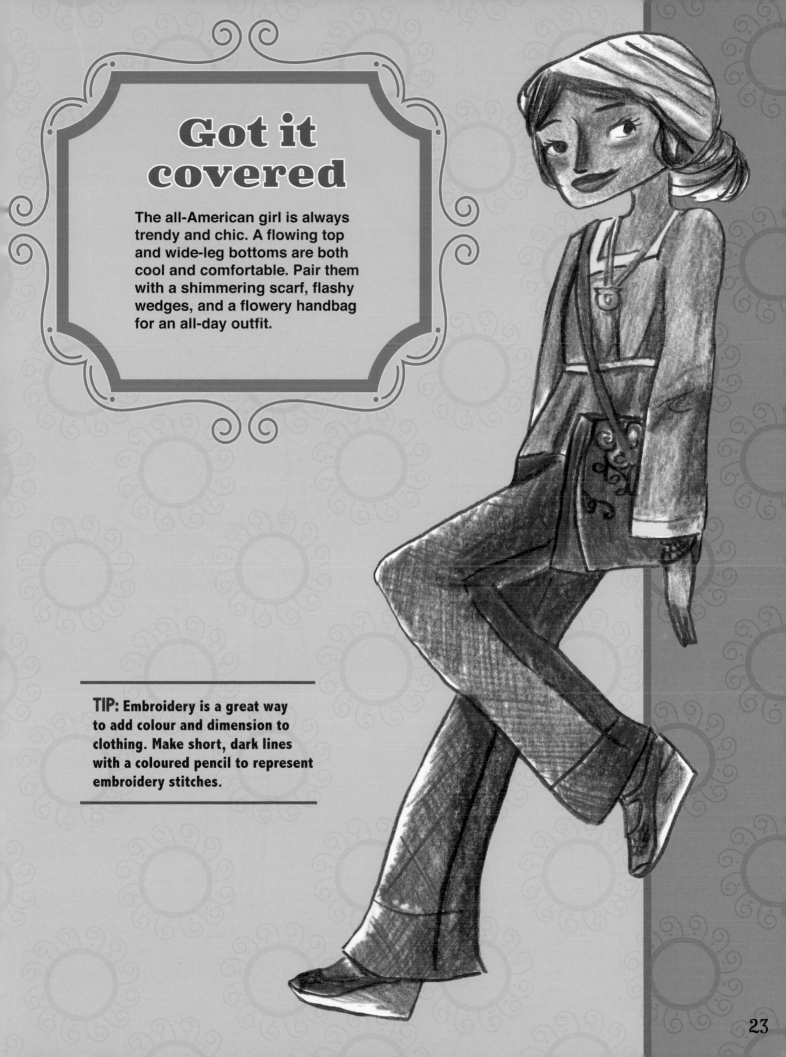

Got it covered

The all-American girl is always trendy and chic. A flowing top and wide-leg bottoms are both cool and comfortable. Pair them with a shimmering scarf, flashy wedges, and a flowery handbag for an all-day outfit.

TIP: Embroidery is a great way to add colour and dimension to clothing. Make short, dark lines with a coloured pencil to represent embroidery stitches.

college COOl

Show the world who you cheer for with your own twist on college style. Stripes, pleats, and argyle patterns are classic combinations for the college-minded fashionista.

TIP: Scarves, foam hands, pompoms, and banners are great accessory additions.

Southwest seasoning

Take in some of the American southwest with rich, natural colours. Native prints, denim accessories, and a touch of amber will spice up any outfit.

TIP: Get inspired! Explore traditional Mexican and American Indian prints for fresh pattern ideas.

INFLUENTIAL PRINTS

Nothing's hotter than African-inspired clothing added to your wardrobe. Sophisticated yet subtle, traditional prints are brought into the next generation of fashion.

TIP: Use a mixture of hot and cool colours and geometric shapes to create a one-of-a-kind print that shows off your style.

Embroidered edges

A simple tiered dress is accented with a splash of colour and some oversized accessories. Colour is minimized, keeping the focus on the dress.

TIP: Use a toothpick or the end of a paintbrush to paint the dots on the dress.

Perfect playsuit

Dresses are great, but sometimes a girly girl needs more freedom. Simple shoes and a sporty jacket dress up this pretty playsuit.

TIP: Use marker over a dry watercolour base to copy the playsuit's floral pattern.

BEACH BOUTIQUE

Take your wardrobe on holiday by turning it tropical. An off-the-shoulder peasant shirt and belted denim shorts are the perfect pair for poolside lounging.

TIP: Lace, ruffles, embroidery, beading, or even sequins will make an even more girly impact.

Pretty prints

Get noticed with bright prints, colourful bangles, and watermelon-coloured wedges. Set the outfit off with a mix of accessories ranging from simple to simply stunning.

TIP: Go beyond geometry by trying out other shapes. Fish, flowers, birds, and fruit are other fun print choices.

Lacy layers

Girly girls know how to use texture to make their style pop. Lace, embroidery, and faux fur create a rugged yet feminine look. A fedora and brogues dress up this easy outfit.

TIP: Use white and light blue coloured pencils over dark blue watercolours or markers. Bold strokes will give the jeans a bright sheen. Short, lighter strokes will make the jeans look more worn.

39

Crocheted cutie

Crochet is a timeless fashion choice for the girly girl. Tights and slouchy grey boots complete a look that's totally casual chic.

TIP: Draw the crochet pattern with white crayon. The crayon wax protects the white paper underneath. Even after being painted over with watercolours, the design stays white. This technique is called resistance painting.

TIMELESS TREND

Step back to the past with a retro party dress. Add a modern twist with a silky clutch and some sassy sunglasses. Pearls and bows are timeless additions in any decade.

TIP: Choose vintage colours for this dress. If you don't like mustard, try powder blue, mint green, canary yellow, or ballet pink.

FLOWERS
are a girl's best friend

Give the girl-next-door image a makeover. A flirty skirt and updated denim add urban appeal. Keep the look sweet with floral and ribbon details.

TIP: Use a hairdryer to warm the tips of the coloured pencils. This will make it easier to blend the layers of the dress.

Style at sea

Don't get swept out to sea looking like a shipwreck. Sweep through first class like you're the captain of fashion.

TIP: A white charcoal pencil will add detail to the hat brim.

Cold weather cool

The only thing warmer than a girly girl's personality is her cool weather gear. Bundle up, but look good doing it! Add plush pieces to create an outfit that's softer than a snowfall.

48

TIP: Soft coloured pencils will give the jeans a natural, washed look.

A vintage affair

Runways around the world have fallen for the Roaring Twenties. Get familiar with the glitz and glamour of the time period. Then add your own modern girly twist.

TIP: Eyeshadow is a good tool to use for anything puffy or furry. Use a foam applicator and cheap eyeshadow to create the soft lines of the bag.

ON THE RUNWAY

TIP: Normal household products make great blending tools. Try:
- nail polish remover
- baby oil
- cotton make-up pads
- cotton swabs
- soft fabric or leather.

A flouncy white dress is ready for the runway on its own. Get more attention with an over-the-top hat and a blended jacket. Fashion week never looked this good.

CUTE KAWAII

In Japanese, "kawaii" means "pretty" or "cute". This fashion style has a sweet, feminine look without being too girly. A ruffled skirt is set off with belts and bows that give this outfit layers of detail.

TIP: Harajuku style is about layers of clothing working together. Make sure each piece works with the others.

Gothic girl

Gothic fashion gained fame in America and the UK in the late 1990s after celebs were seen sporting black outfits. But Gothic style in Japan was already famous, and is very different. Girlishness and innocence are themes Japanese Goths like to feature.

TIP: Don't get distracted by dark colours. Goth girls are cute and confident!

CYBERPUNK *show-off*

Cyberpunk style was first featured in *FRUiTS*, a Japanese fashion magazine, in the late 1990s. This style, which combines technology and Gothic fashion, makes the space age look sweet.

TIP: Bright colours, wild prints, and unusual materials bring out the sci-fi side of Harajuku.

Baby, you're sweet

Frills, lace, and bows are part of the most well-known Harajuku style, known as Loli. A modernized take on elegant, vintage clothing, Loli style brings antique dolls to life.

TIP: Use dark colours instead of light to turn this into a Goth-Loli look.

VISUAL-KEI

Japanese rock bands began adopting the popular Goth-Loli look. Then they incorporated their wardrobes into their music. This style-to-song crossover is called visual-kei.

TIP: In Japanese, visual-kei translates to "visual music style". Extreme make-up and costumes match the dark, creepy music they pair with.

Decora'd out

Short for "decoration", decora is the most colourful Harajuku style. A rainbow of hues, hairclips, and lots of layers make decora dressers stand out in a crowd.

TIP: Decora is a great style to practise using a variety of colours and tones. Try using a combination of coloured pencils, markers, and crayons.

Elegant Loli

Emphasize the Goth half of Goth-Loli with serious colours and romantic ruffles. Ribbons, bows, frills, curls, and lace make a dark, Gothic outfit soft and flirty.

TIP: The layers and frills of this outfit are perfect for practising shading techniques.

MIXED TRADITIONS

The origin of Harajuku style was the combination of traditional Japanese clothing with western style. Some call this style "wamono". Kimonos are updated with fashionable fabrics and prints. Modern accessories finish the crossover between past and present.

TIP: Go crazy with prints! Animal prints, tartans, polka dots, ginghams, and floral patterns will set off this original outfit.

MR URA-HARA

"Ura" means "under" in Japanese. The name *Ura-Hara* signifies the reserved, underground aspect of this Harajuku style. Ura-Hara is a combination of hip-hop, graffiti, and skater trends. It is Harajuku's take on male fashion.

TIP: Keep your outfits stylish with clean lines and simple pieces. Use limited colour and patterns. Instead, try using unusual fabrics and textures, such as animal fur, spray paint, and metals.

Sweet as a Loli-pop

Pair the lovely look of Loli with bubblegum pink decora. Combining the two styles creates the cutest kawaii outfit ever! There's no such thing as too much pink when you're sweet as a Loli-pop.

TIP: This outfit will test your creativity! How many accessory pieces can you add before you can't think of any more?

TAKE IT TO THE STREET

A true Harajuku wearer is comfortable standing out in a crowd. Take it to the street by combining punk, kawaii, decora, and visual-kei styles. You'll be stepping out in a one-of-a-kind outfit.

TIP: Experiment with a small combination of colours to find complementary groupings. Try blue, teal, black, and white, or red, purple, white, and yellow.

Belle of the disco ball

Dance the night away with a flowing chiffon dress. The blending of colour creates a unique, one-of-a-kind gown that shines both on and off the dance floor.

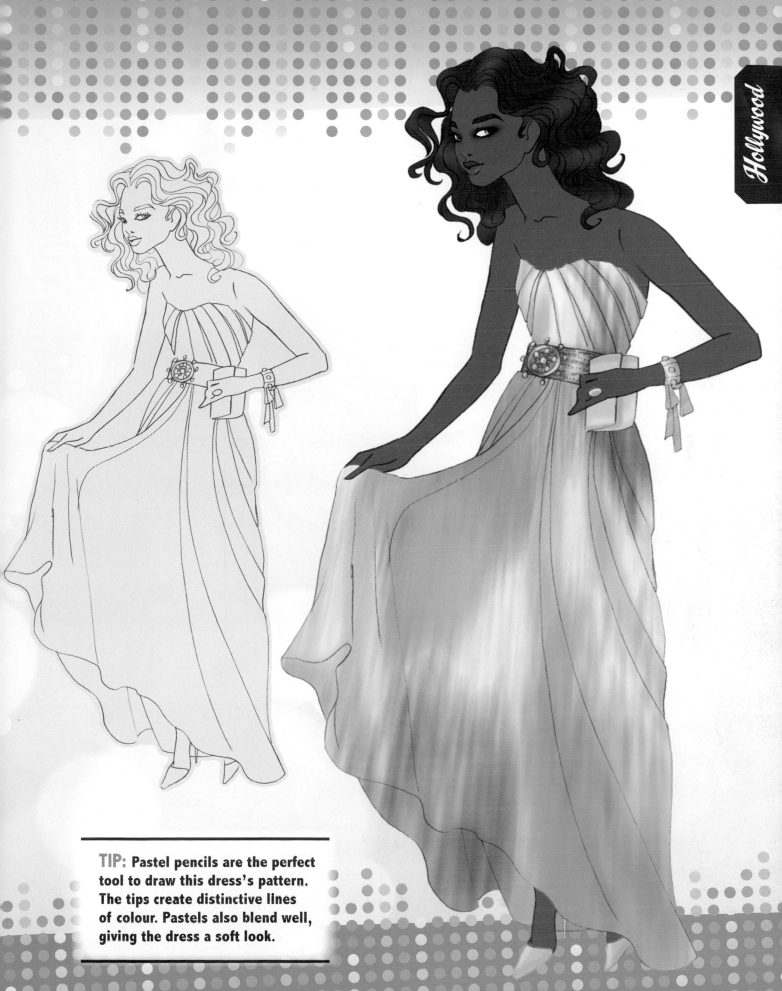

TIP: Pastel pencils are the perfect tool to draw this dress's pattern. The tips create distinctive lines of colour. Pastels also blend well, giving the dress a soft look.

Short and sweet

Ring in the new year with party poppers, fireworks, and a rocking party dress. Your only resolution should be to look this good next year too!

TIP: This dress's simplicity means it's great to experiment with. Give charcoal or graphite pencils a try instead of the usual coloured pencils or markers.

Red carpet ruffles

Catch the camera's attention while walking the red carpet. Shining ruffles will catch the paparazzi's eye and make the front-page news.

TIP: A metallic marker or white graphite pencil will help the dress shine.

Outshine any award with a dress as fluid as liquid metal. Nothing goes with a gold statue like a molten metal dress.

TIP: Use watercolours to colour the dress. Sprinkle salt onto wet watercolour wherever you want to add shine. Once the paint has dried, carefully brush off the salt. The salt will create the textured effect on the dress.

STAR-STUDDED SHEATH

A sheath dress flatters most body types. This style also adds a touch of old-fashioned elegance to any formal event. While no necklace is needed, chandelier earrings bring just the right touch of glam.

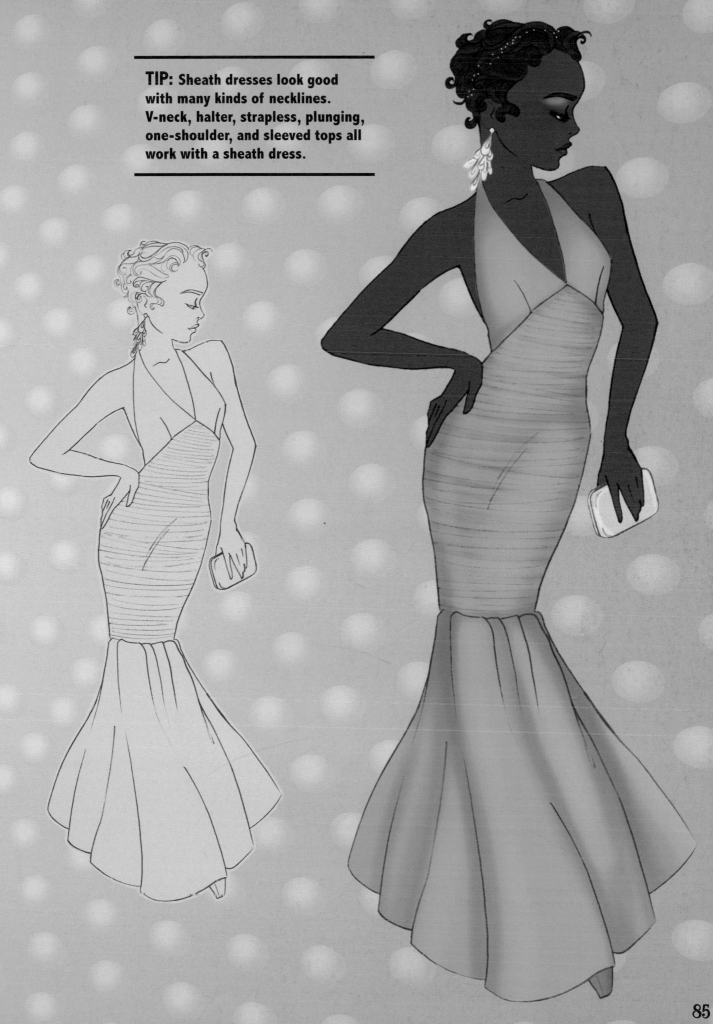

TIP: Sheath dresses look good with many kinds of necklines. V-neck, halter, strapless, plunging, one-shoulder, and sleeved tops all work with a sheath dress.

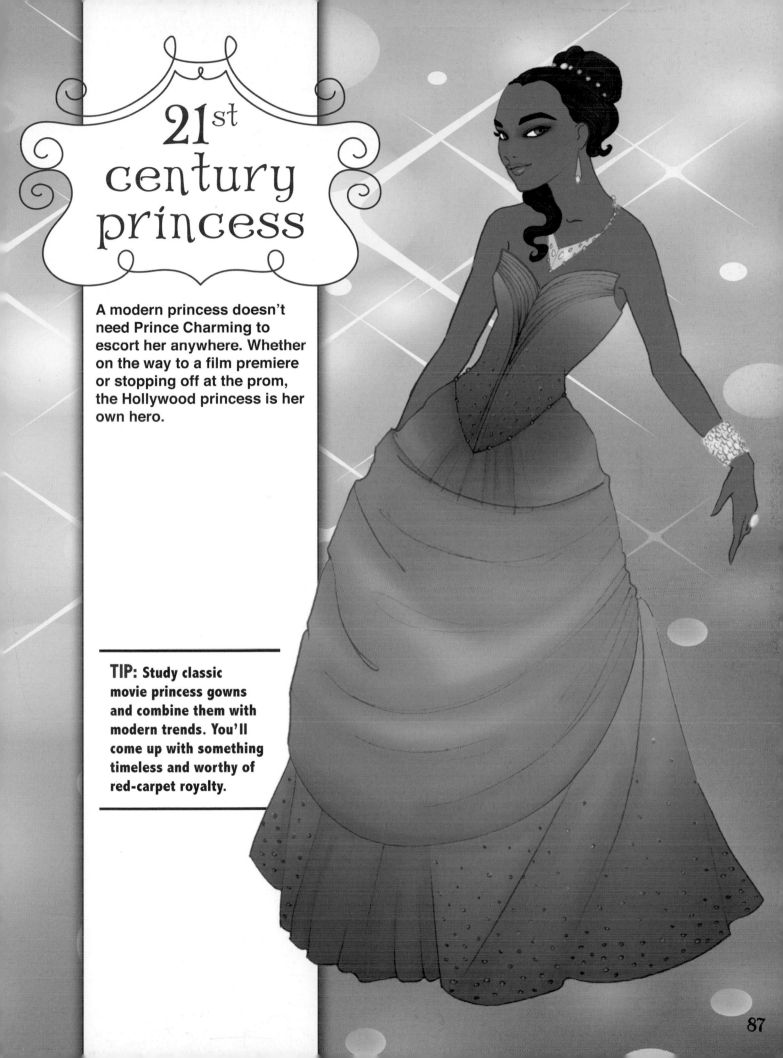

21st century princess

A modern princess doesn't need Prince Charming to escort her anywhere. Whether on the way to a film premiere or stopping off at the prom, the Hollywood princess is her own hero.

TIP: Study classic movie princess gowns and combine them with modern trends. You'll come up with something timeless and worthy of red-carpet royalty.

Floral formal

Who needs a corsage when you've brought your own bouquet? Roses are seen as a symbol of love and beauty, and you should too.

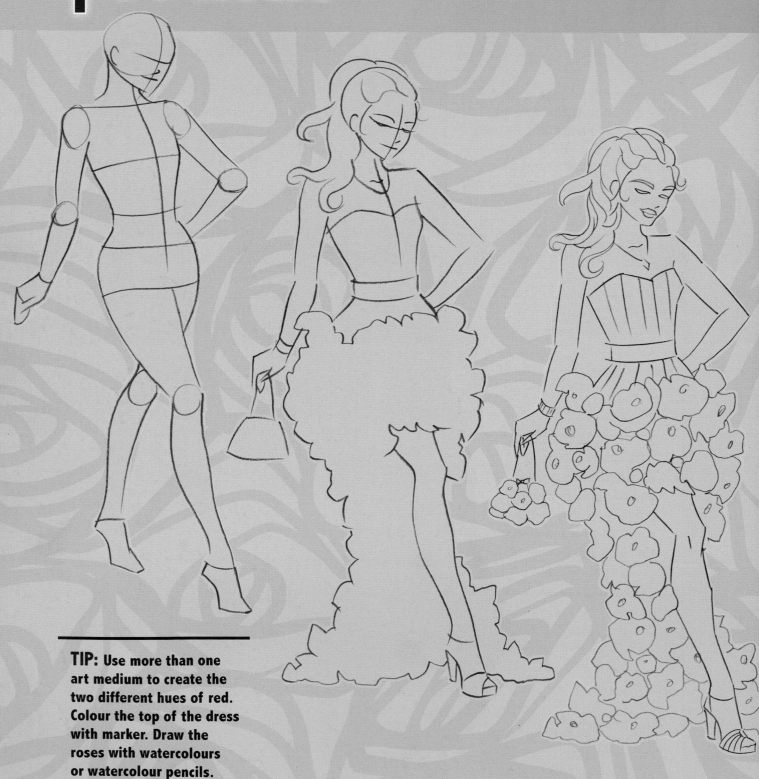

TIP: Use more than one art medium to create the two different hues of red. Colour the top of the dress with marker. Draw the roses with watercolours or watercolour pencils.

Hall of famer

TIP: Stick to simple colours for the accessories. The dress is colourful enough on its own.

A rocker in the hall of fame has reached the height of stardom! Dress like you're at the top even if you're still on the waiting list. This outfit will dazzle any crowd.

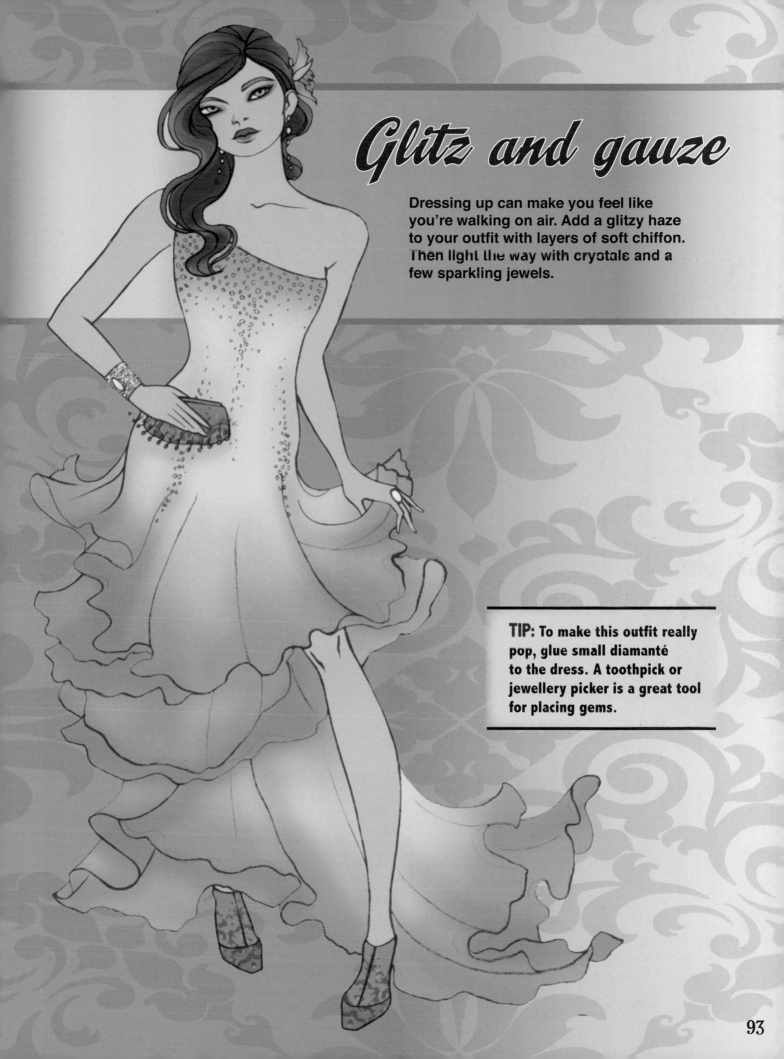

Glitz and gauze

Dressing up can make you feel like you're walking on air. Add a glitzy haze to your outfit with layers of soft chiffon. Then light the way with crystals and a few sparkling jewels.

TIP: To make this outfit really pop, glue small diamanté to the dress. A toothpick or jewellery picker is a great tool for placing gems.

BackStage GLAM

Presenters and musical acts are essential to the success of any awards show. Get the audience cheering for an encore with this fabulous dress.

TIP: Use a thin-tipped black, blue, or silver permanent marker to outline the dress's layers.

Think pink

Being a starlet is all about youth and energy. Act your age in a short sweetheart dress with a ruffled hemline. A contrasting chiffon scarf catches the eye and adds a pop of colour.

TIP: Use watercolours for the dress. While the paint is wet, add colour to the skirt. Once the paint is dry, paint the jewels onto the bodice.

TIP: If you find you like Asian-inspired dresses, add them to your sketchbook. Use Asian prints to add a twist to the ordinary prom dress.

ASIAN INSPIRED

Dress designs and prints from around the world freshen up the formal scene. Traditional Japanese clothing lends itself to bright colours and modern prints. Updated accessories, such as hair ornaments and umbrellas, are tickets to the international stage.

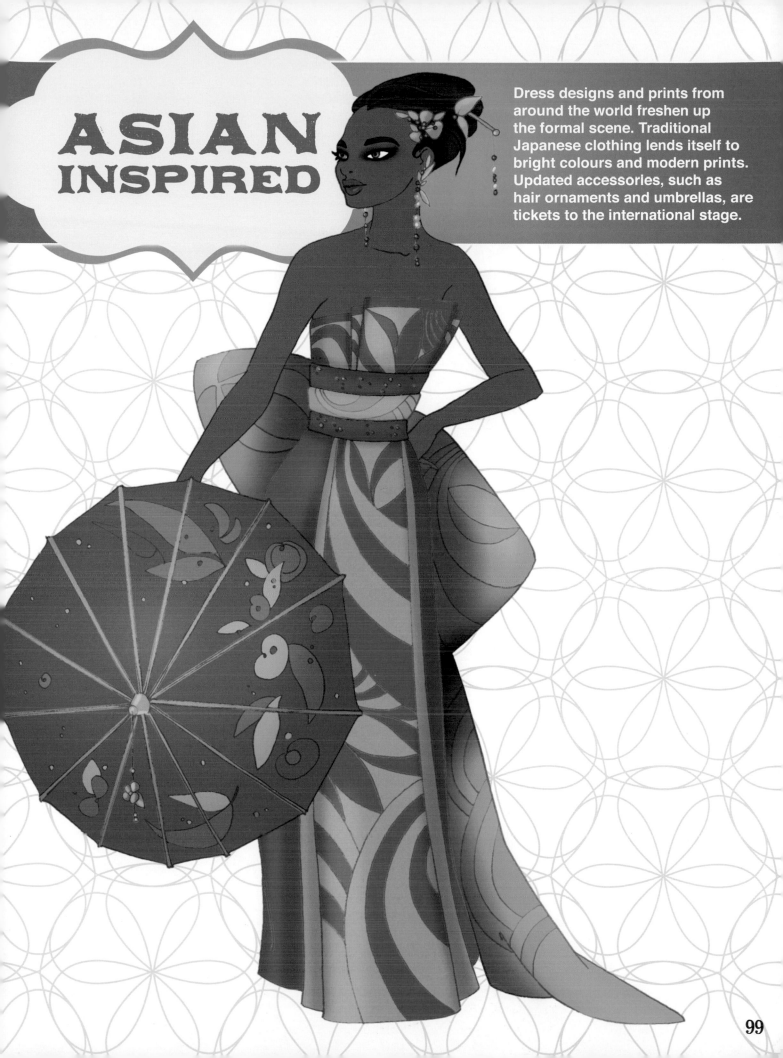

POWER BALLAD

Animal prints and ripped denim have been fashion picks for rock stars of any era. Rock the ages with these timeless threads.

TIP: Use whites and very light blues to recreate distressed denim.

SCHOOL OF ROCK

Dress for success at the school of hard knocks. Bring some rock star flair to the boring world of suits and ties. Red accents bring this outfit to a whole new level.

TIP: When it comes to red, a little can go a long way. Use it to enhance the outfit's colours without letting it take over.

Little Miss METALHEAD

Steal the show with big splashes of colour. Accessories are what makes this outfit pop. Belts, bangles, and boots hold everything together.

TIP: Metallic tones help the accessories in this outfit stand out. Try using metallic paint instead of ordinary pens for a look that shines.

LET'S SHRED

Rock stars have to look good anytime, anywhere. Paparazzi could be waiting around any corner! Take style over the edge with a shredded dress and spikes to match.

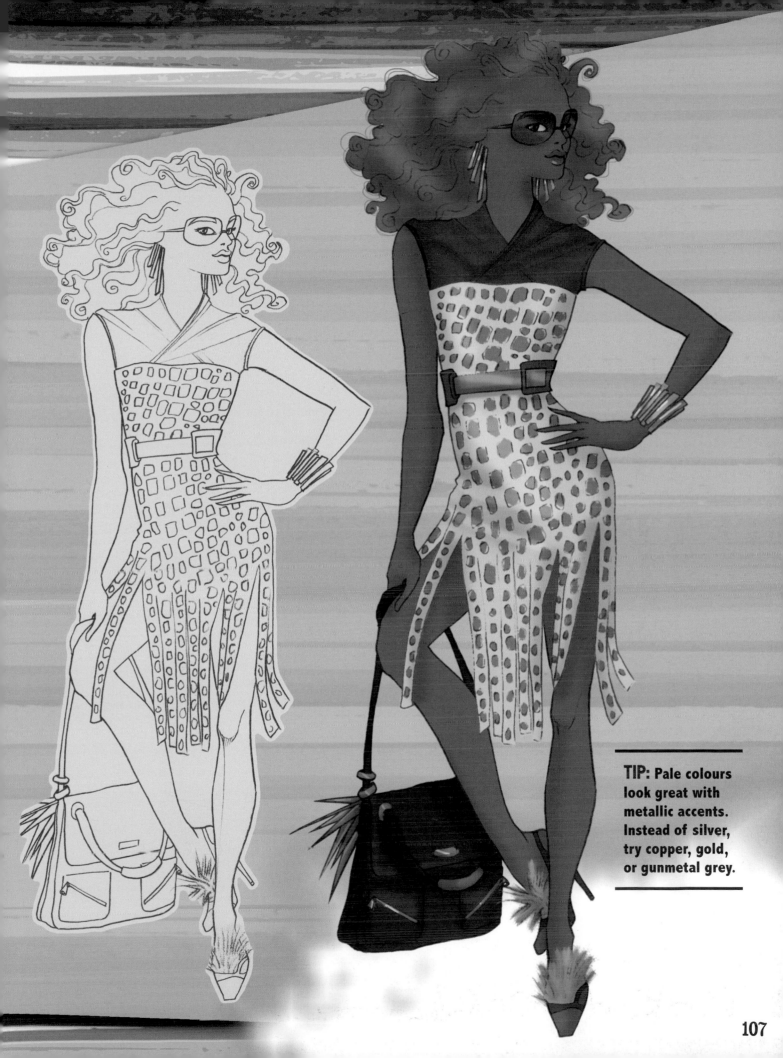

TIP: Pale colours look great with metallic accents. Instead of silver, try copper, gold, or gunmetal grey.

CROSSOVER ARTIST

Launch the rock star wardrobe to new levels with a fresh look. Keep rocker cred with military-inspired style and bright colours. Checks lend a touch of everyday fashion to the look.

TIP: Glow-in-the-dark paint will add an extreme effect to the boots and top.

Some become stars by twists of fate. Others are born famous. Rock royalty dresses like there's a concert happening every night.

TIP: Give the jacket a real leather look by using soft matt colours.

HARD ROCK RIFFS

Storm the stage with star power! Zips, spikes, and metal feel feminine with the addition of purple and bright green. Sing your heart out, and shout your style out loud.

TIP: Coloured pencils, pastels, or thin permanent markers will help the tartan trousers pop.

SOFT METAL

Not all rock stars love studs and metal. Some stars have a softer shine! Add some truly girly flair with a ruffled skirt and a lace top.

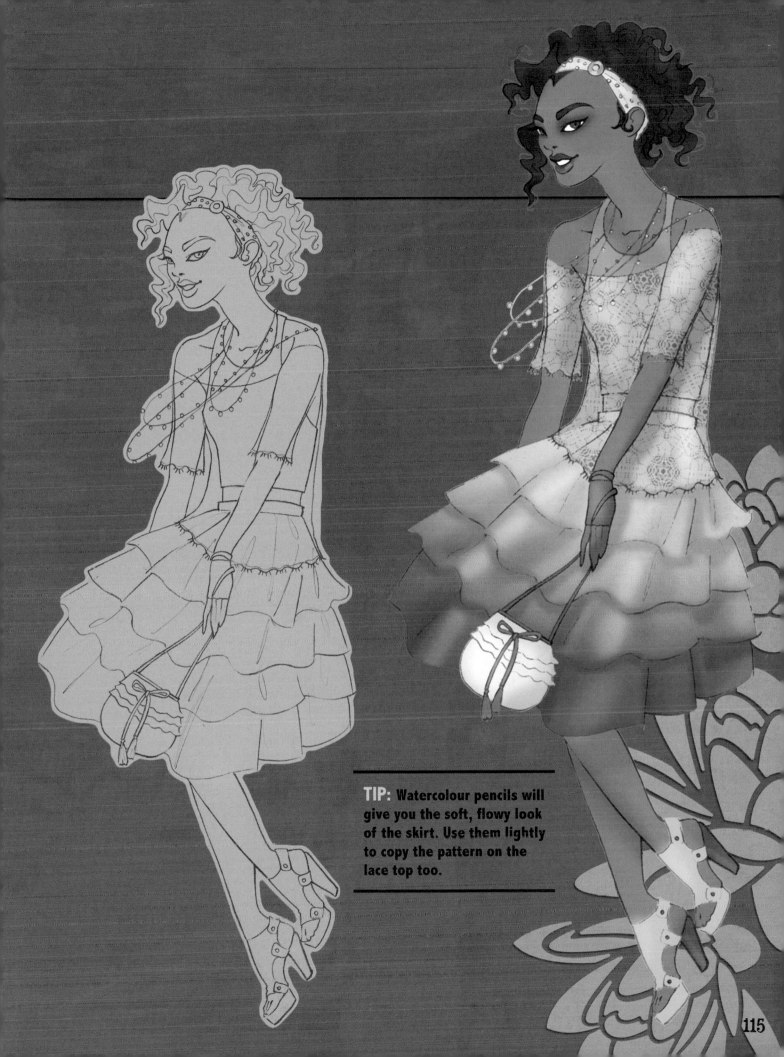

TIP: Watercolour pencils will give you the soft, flowy look of the skirt. Use them lightly to copy the pattern on the lace top too.

COVER ARTIST

Choosing a great outfit is as important to a rock star as picking a great song. Killer accessories ensure this collection is more than a one-hit wonder.

TIP: Go wild with patterns! If plain trousers aren't your thing, experiment with animal prints, bold stripes, or bright graphics.

Country solo

Go back to the country with a cowgirl-inspired outfit. Linen, leather, and country-girl sass guarantee a classic style with added attitude!

TIP: For extra impact, use a silver pen to add small studs to the jacket. Or add swirly lines to the boots with a turquoise marker.

PARTY IN THE DARK

Light up the night in a neon-inspired gown. The bright rings will guarantee that this rock star's glow doesn't go out.

TIP: Use a scratchboard with rainbow colours underneath for a realistic effect. Etch the design onto the scratchboard. The rainbow colours will make up the lines of the dress.

Back to basics

Start simple with blue jeans and layered vests. Stick to relaxed-fit clothing and sensible accessories. The skater chic style is all about being comfortable in what you wear.

TIP: Use shading to add creases and depth to the tops and jeans.

VERT STYLE

A baseball cap, boyfriend sweater, and awesome jeans are all you need to reach the height of skater chic.

TIP: Vary the pressure you use with watercolour pencils to create the look of these one-of-a-kind jeans.

STREET LEAGUE STYLE

The skater boy is as casual as they come. He's ready to hang with friends on the sidelines or gain big air in a halfpipe. Fashion stays on the down-low with street league style.

TIP: Checks make a great pattern for experimenting with colour. Try colour combinations that you haven't used before.

127

SKATER PREP

Educate yourself at skater school while looking stylish too. Put a spin on ordinary tartan by adding an underlayer of taffeta and an overlayer of silver chains.

TIP: Try using a cotton bud to soften the lines for a more natural look. Moisten the cotton bud for a more blended pattern.

SURF SKATER

When skater girls need sun, they hit the beach and surf the boardwalk! Wave to the crowd in style while wearing natural tones of the earth and sea.

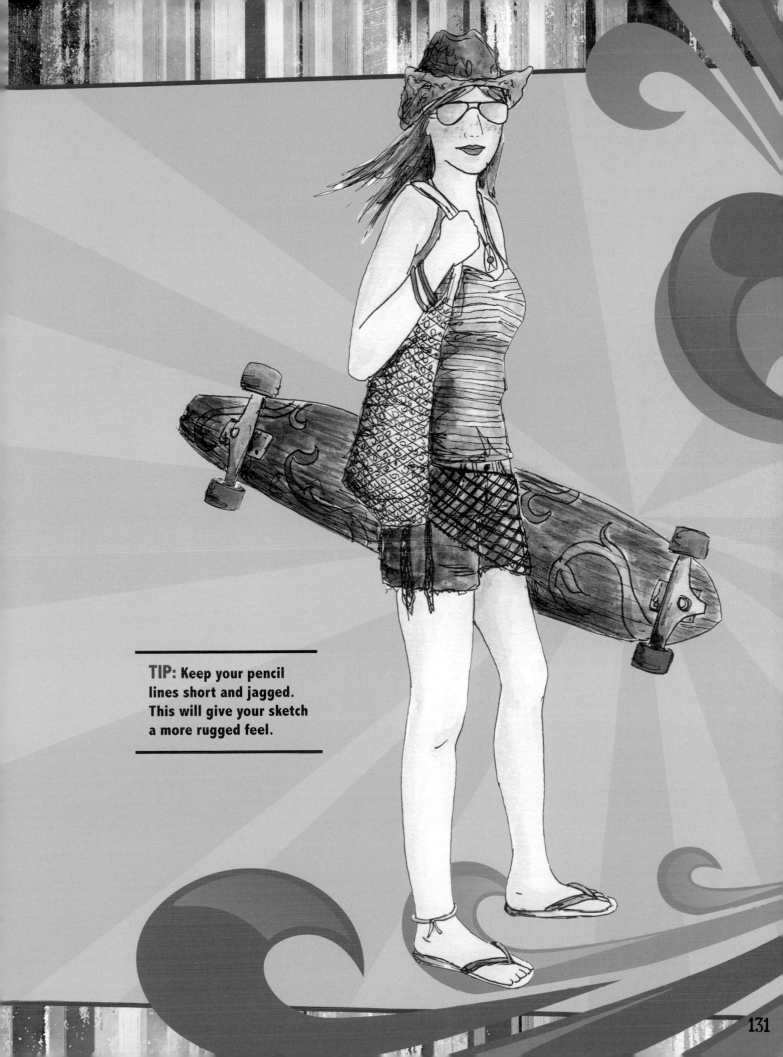

TIP: Keep your pencil lines short and jagged. This will give your sketch a more rugged feel.

Hanging out

Get relaxed with skater chic casual wear. Dress up familiar jeans with a super stylish hoody. Add coordinating sunglasses and a tasselled bag. Then top things off with a knitted hat. Hanging out never looked so good!

TOP DECK STYLE

Skater guys have a sense of style too!
Keep it simple with casual trousers and
a T-shirt. Give the outfit a personal twist
with a colourful coat, a pair of funky shoes,
and a bright belt.

TIP: With its simple lines, this outfit can be tailored to fit your own personal style.

Overall impression

Skater girls don't spend all day at the skate park. For more dressy occasions, a sundress, boots, and denim jacket will take the stylish skater anywhere she pleases.

TIP: Use watercolour pencils to create the dress print. Colour in the pattern, and then brush gently with a wet paintbrush. Once the pattern is dry, use a black pen to add more texture.

TIP: Try using the watercolour pencils on a wet surface. See which technique you like best.

137

Supertech sparkle

Get ready to go out by adding a shimmery sparkle. Start with an animal print skirt as a centrepiece. Then add a few pieces of interest that catch the eye.

TIP: Experiment with
texture! Glue down a piece
of fabric in place of the
skirt. Or use glitter glue
for some 3-D shine.

1080 winter wear

Staying warm while gliding through snow is important. Looking good while doing it is also key! Turn heads on the hill with gear that's snowboarder chic.

TIP: Practise creating cool graphics using paint and markers. Snowboards are great canvases for street-inspired art.

At the PARK

Dress to impress at the skate park!
Lace-up boots, a practical-but-fashionable
outfit, and a helmet will get you noticed.
Grab a board, and you're ready to go.

TIP: Turn safety gear into an accessory! Coordinate outfits with helmets, goggles, gloves, and protective pads.

Raintree is an imprint of Capstone Global Library Limited, incorporated in England and Wales having its registered office at 7 Pilgrim Street, London, EC4V 6LB – Registered company number: 6695582

To contact Raintree:
Phone: 0845 6044371
Fax: + 44 (0) 1865 312263
Email: myorders@raintreepublishers.co.uk
Outside the UK please telephone +44 1865 312262.

First published by © Capstone Young Readers in 2013
First published in the United Kingdom in 2014
The moral rights of the proprietor have been asserted.

All rights reserved. No part of this publication may be reproduced in any form or by any means (including photocopying or storing it in any medium by electronic means and whether or not transiently or incidentally to some other use of this publication) without the written permission of the copyright owner, except in accordance with the provisions of the Copyright, Designs and Patents Act 1988 or under the terms of a licence issued by the Copyright Licensing Agency, Saffron House, 6–10 Kirby Street, London EC1N 8TS (www.cla.co.uk). Applications for the copyright owner's written permission should be addressed to the publisher.

Written by: Mari Bolte
Illustrated by:
Sole Otero (All-American Girl)
Brooke Hagel (Girly Girl and Harajuku)
Sarah Dahl (Hollywood and Rock Star)
Jennifer Rzasa (Skater Chic)
Designed by: Lori Bye
Art Director: Nathan Gassman
Production Specialist: Laura Manthe
Printed and bound in China

ISBN 978 1 4062 6642 9
17 16 15 14 13
10 9 8 7 6 5 4 3 2 1

British Library Cataloguing in Publication Data
A full catalogue record for this book is available from the British Library.